The GIFT

messages from frog crossing

four seasons of haiku and senryu

About HAIKU . . .

Japanese in origin, this genre is centuries old. It started as a parlor game. Translations of Basho, the father of haiku, Buson, Issa, Shiti and other seventeenth century haikuists can be found in most libraries.

Japanese art generally follows a strict regimen; haiku is no exception. Traditionally, in Japanese, haiku is terse-verse containing 3 lines of 5-7-5 onji. Onji is the Japanese measure of sound. Our closest counterpart is the syllable. Yet since these two aren't the same, many modern American haikuists don't hesitate to use fewer syllables still employing the short/long/short format. They feel it more closely reflects the essence of haiku. As you will see that is often my style.

The subject of haiku is nature. Because haiku is always written in the present tense, the here and now, we see the future as an illusion—the past a memory—leaving only the moment. That fleeting aesthetic moment almost always contains a season reference enabling the reader to instantly grasp the weather, the foliage, and the emotions invoked, which is all important to the poem in the spirit of word economy. Often two unrelated elements are juxtaposed. In this almost non-poem, the haikuist remains invisible.

In writing haiku, we relate what we see and not what we think, taking care not to let words get between us and the image. Haiku is spontaneous and suggestive and may evoke and immediate intuitive reaction, a revelation, an "Ah-ha!" from the reader. In it's evocative incompleteness, the reader is allowed to rhapsodize.

OFTEN, THERE IS A SENSE OF WABI, A SPIRIT WHICH FINDS THE BIG IN THE SMALL, THE BEAUTIFUL IN THE SIMPLE. HAIKU INSISTS ON SENSITIVE AND TRUTHFUL OBSERVATIONS—EVEN THE ILLUSIONS MUST BE ACCURATE. IN ITS SIMPLICITY, THERE ARE NO SIMILES OR METAPHORS, AND FEW ADJECTIVES. A SUBTLE SABI ELEMENT, A TINGE OF MELANCHOLY, SOMETIMES SHADOWS A HAIKU.

ABOUT SENRYU

THE HAIKU IN THIS BOOK ARE INTERLACED WITH SENRYU. FOR MANY HAIKU POETS, SENRYU COMES AS A RESULT FROM WRITING HAIKU.

MUCH LIKE HAIKU IN FORM, SENRYU DIFFERS IN TONE AND IS ABOUT HUMAN NATURE RATHER THAN NATURE. THE POET MAY NOT BE QUITE SO INVISIBLE AS HE PROBES HUMAN EMOTIONS. SENRYU RELATES TO EVERYDAY TRUTHS, HAPPY OR SAD, SOMETIMES IRONIC, OFTEN HUMOROUS. SOME OF MY HAIKU FRIENDS THINK SENRYU IS MORE FUN. BOTH HAIKU AND SENRYU DEAL WITH THAT MOMENT OF AWARENESS. ALTHOUGH THERE IS NO CHOOSING ONE FORM OVER THE OTHER, I FEEL INTERSPERSING HAIKU WITH SENRYU ENHANCES BOTH.

OUR CULTURE AND LANGUAGE ARE SO VASTLY DIFFERENT FROM THE JAPANESE, THAT AFTER MORE THAN THIRTY YEARS OF "PLAYING AROUND" WITH THIS GENRE, I CONSIDER MY HAIKU AND SENRYU MODERNIZED, AMERICANIZED AND ADELIZED.

ONE OF MY FAVORITE PLACES IS THE OREGON COAST; ONE OF MY FAVORITE HAIKU RESULTED FROM VACATIONING THERE.

WALKING THE BEACH AT DAYBREAK, DENSE FOG ROLLED OFF THE PACIFIC. I COULDN'T SEE MY HANDS IN FRONT OF MY FACE. IT WAS AS THOUGH THE BLACKBOARD OF EARTH HAD SUDDENLY BEEN WIPED CLEAN. I EXPERIENCED A FEELING OF BEING SUSPENDED IN SPACE—UNEARTHED.

THEN, SLOWLY, A PARTIAL IMAGE OF HAYSTACK ROCK, IN ALL ITS SPLENDOR, JUTTING FROM THE SEA, MATERIALIZED. ONE OF LIFE'S PERFECT MOMENTS.

OUT OF THE FOG
THE EARTH INVENTS ITSELF
ROCK BY ROCK

For *JACK*

-and-

For the supportive spirits in Poetry Workshop: **Frances Reid, Pat Litz, Ann Vycital, Sylvia LaMoyne, Marjorie Koch, Deanne Tawney, Leonard Field and Joe Glymour.**

-also-

Elizabeth Blaine, Ann Vycital, Betty Penson Ward, for validating my efforts

Don Holtson, *Author of Haiku, Reading It, Writing It,* for editing the introduction

-and-

David Priebe, Editor, *Haiku Headlines and Timepieces,* **Robert Spiess,** Editor, *Modern Haiku,* **Lorraine Ellis Harr,** Editor, *Dragonfly,* **Francine Porad,** Editor, *Brussels Sprout,* **Jim Kacian,** Editor, *Frogpond,* **Chuck Easter,** Editor, *black bough,* **Lora Homan Zill,** Editor, *Time of Singing and Psalms and Serenades, a celebration of Idaho Poets,* for their inspiring publications and for publishing my haiku and senryu.

-and-

To the very talented artists whose work appears between these covers

Jan Van Schuyler, *Boise, Idaho,* WINTER PINK, *a watercolor*

Sydney Johnson, *Boise, Idaho,* THE OREGON COAST, *a watercolor*

Dr. Xiao Xiang Sun, *Beijing, China,* GUILIN, *a watercolor*

Pat Rutledge, *Tacoma, Washington,* NIGHT HERON, *a batik*

**

sketches by Adelaide

open yourself to the beauty of life

There is no more appropriate title for this book than:

THE GIFT

As each new day is a gift in itself, haiku is the gift that brings new
awareness into focus, enriching life as we connect with
the universe, touch the spiritual and
live in the Now.
Here is *THE GIFT.* It is for you.

Warning: Haiku may become addictive although not harmful to your health

Coffee Table Books

in

the

park

our

favorite

picnic

bench

occupied

by

snow

we are all part of the great design

in his stocking cap
catching snowflakes on his tongue
. . . the taste of winter

the card list still grows
never can find an old friend
to forget

blanket of snow
smothering the creek bed
silence

down asphalt pavement
pools of color washing
night rain bleeds neon

late to bed
he rolls over to give me
the warm spot

catching the fever
we wander the mall   shopping
for the miracle

yule decorations
downtown traffic lights blinking
red then green

web-work of bare limbs
against a red morning sky
fine lace for Christmas

day before Christmas
under the tree   packages
growing deeper

on the tree
plastic ornaments
child-high

snow-covered field
   a flock of blackbirds
      beading the power line

                              snowfall challenging
                              luminary serpentine
                                 flames flutter

nine-year old
upside-down reading
the package tags

                                in darkness
                     Christmas lights gift-wrapping
                              the snow

the five year old --
 "if it's Jesus's birthday
--where's the cake?"

                                that crass crow
                     perches on a sign that reads
                            "NO PARKING"

Christmas morning
last summer's huckleberries
in breakfast waffles

opening her gifts
the little girl counting
her brother's

the family has grown
how easy now to hold hands
around the table

little children
on their best behavior
struggle with goblets

post-dinner duet
man of the house and his dog
snoring together

telephoned to ask
"who was it with Alzheimer's?"
---- couldn't remember

reading his paper
nothing can disturb this man
. . . but demanding bark

dawn comes brighter
the earth illuminated
newly fallen snow

a raft of new toys
children arguing over
the old tire swing

blind German Shepherd
navigating the road with
seeing-eye boy

Christmas boxed away
in the dumps, discarded tree
the wrappings   me

same time   every day
  man who used to walk his dog
    walks his shadow

      January walk . . .
    looking at her icy words
      hanging in the air

      a frigid wind
  and a gloomy woman
    coming in the door

      a thousand diamonds
    etching the winter window
      --drafty single pane

sparrow in the snow
embossing a design
with tiny feet

wet   smelly
sad eyes begging
at the door

on-coming headlights
as the snow intensifies
our muscles tighten

no child support
he aborts his six-year-old
this pro-lifer

out the car window
the dog's nose nuzzling
the wind

church parking lot sign
"we forgive your trespasses
. . . but we'll have you towed"

the sick bed
her tears running down
his cheek

family album
distinguished-looking man
no one remembers

hesitating
last pair of high heels
in the goodwill box

pigeons flying
high in the misty sky
that absorbs them

brisk morning walk
meadowlark's call shattering
silence of winter

playing with grandma
little boy hiding himself
---can't hide his giggle

brittle with cold
old man walks gingerly
down icy steps

footprints on the steps
quickly filling with snowflakes
erase his visit

near the pub
crows gather in the tree-tops
before they head home

a deep freeze morning
under the hood of the car
a stray cat crouching

fog vertigo
feel skis giving away
. . . and then the earth

morning mist
sun masquerading
as the moon

icicles tug
at the worn-out awning
of summers past

smell of corn popping . . .
the loneliness of winter
melting like butter

five o'clock traffic
cars pulled in all directions
by magnet called "home"

February
fence posts in the fields
growing shorter

melting snowman
seeps into the thawing earth
where does the white go?

mist of the lake
smearing the far horizon
where black and white meet

on the state house lawn
flock of crows convening
with the legislators

precious little hands
clinging to my shoulder
and my heartstrings

two-year-old
offers a heart-shaped cookie
then takes a bite

spring nudging winter
snow patches in the meadow
edged with buttercups

little feet can't reach
the pedals — little legs
suddenly grow

just at twilight
deep in the river marsh
a night heron stirs

Just when I thought I was getting some place

old turf turning green
in the forgotten place
. . hides the epitaph

in melting snow bank
a bush of pussy willows
wears new fur mittens

little rascal
takes his new dress shoes
puddle-walking

helium balloon
in the sky   string waves
"good-bye"

13

under the elm
a drift of violets
suddenly appear

spring clean-up   bonfire
once more autumn's flaming leaves
return to color

the first sunny day
sidewalk piled with little shoes
barefoot in the grass

a gusty March day
wishing for a little boy
to fly this kite

clock ticks
do it! do it! do it!
moment disappears

outside the window
chirping comes from a new nest
announcing the dawn

wind chimes
almost playing
a tune

on a barbed-wire fence
a crow spreads his wings
calligraphically

under dry leaves
long-awaited crocus blooms
unseen

one tiny puddle
in the big church parking lot
his dress shoes find it

flowing rhythm
feeling the crescendo swell
rafting white water

against dry reeds
having to look twice to see
the Great Blue Heron

no restaurant sign
generous wafts of garlic
tell it's Italian

from the fertile earth
hoe releasing the musky smell
a hint of roses

in the unmown lawn
almost unnoticed
. . . scattered violets

beggar on the steps
passer-by diverts her eyes
like he isn't there

old discarded pot
recycles itself this spring with
a dandelion

braking!
sudden cross-traffic
monstrous bird shadows

against the wetlands
the swollen river rages
-- a blue heron flies

bloom opening
wet butterfly wings
unfolding

after the rain
a wren flies to her nest
the willows shine

under April skies
long johns dance on the clothesline
-- the country two-step

in the garden shop
a yellow smudge on her nose
she buys a lily

a fish jumps
swelling circles disappear
taking my thought

brushing the dog
just in time for the wren
to line her nest

the magpie
though he wears a tuxedo
he has no class

among plum blossoms
a string of Christmas lights
tree for all seasons

car out in the rain
baby robins nesting on
---the door opener

mixing the colors
is politically correct
planting petunias

a covey of quail
darting across the roadway
as though connected

at the feed store
a flock of vagrant ducks
outside quacking

in the high country
a meadow of blue camas
repeating the sky

through the fog
a bush of lilac blossoms
in watercolor

as the sun goes down
white-haired women tote flowers
among old tombstones

hollow sound echoes
against the silence of dawn
woodpecker is back

suddenly slowing
the bustle of traffic
magnolia in bloom

after the storm
raindrops on the window
capture the sun

wet with spring
a row of purple tulips
kowtow to the east

mergansers --
chicks pile on mama's back
the lake roughens

last baby robin
on the edge of the pine bough
wide-eyed   trembling

under the stars
around the cold campfire
prolong the moment

there   in plain view
a doe   invisible
then her ears twitch

a field of mustard
the magnitude of yellow
. . . explaining the taste

threads of light
driving night shadows back
in the corners

23

whispering
silences
the crowd

can't throw it away
letter to her late husband
can't forward it

dancing frantically
to the sounds of the night wind
shadows on the wall

morning in the park
the grass greening   trees leafing
homeless sleeping

the church garden
rows of pure white lilies
genuflecting

in midnight stillness
bonfire smoke climbs pencil straight
up to the moon

caught in a wind draft
the seagull suspended
motionless

hidden in the leaves
the melodious song of
an unknown bird

as darkness falls
one lone goose overhead
--- announcing it

the river swells
closer to our door now
the mergansers

the wind   kindly
sweeping a pile of dry leaves
off the porch

cling possessively
to the cottage door
wisteria

walking carefully
   on the elegance
      fallen plum blossoms

after heavy rain
fairy umbrellas pop up
   on the forest floor

on Mother's Day
three grown men bringing home
 . . . their childhood

just before the storm
sky-full of dappled stallions
   --their thundering hoofs

children all tucked in --
watching from the porch swing
   wren flies to her nest

enough!
pulling weeds all day long
now in my dreams

Japanese maple
leaves unfolding
like a fan

from the air balloon
the people down below
diminishing

in darkness
even the cricket's voice
sounds lonely

separated
yet forever bound
by this child

one more luncheon guest
from the floral centerpiece
an earwig crawling

leaves falling
on the azalea
as buds form

deserted school grounds
just a little boy jumping
--- into his shadow

eating breakfast
eye-contact with a squirrel
eating his

novice gardener
cared for a seedling that grew
to be a milkweed

hushed whispering
walking through the deep forest
reverently

wilderness trek
leaving only footprints
taking memories

in the morning fog
tide unfurls releasing
. . . . some seagulls

faded and dusty
these artificial flowers
don't know how to wilt

a white butterfly
in this field of daisies
--keeps disappearing

from the campfire
sun sinks into the lake
. . . hear it sizzle!

in the sleeping bag
listening to the frogs croak
wishing they would croak

shooing the water
back into the ocean
a sandpiper

silky silver threads
crocheted in a star-burst
moonlit spider web

barely a breeze
a milkweed parachuting
-- to new digs

roaring tide breaks
against the rocky shoreline
scattering moonbeams

tall shadows
all night they hum their mantra
the ponderosa

pent-up anger
enjoying each hard snip
of the pruning shears

a little bird
that flew against the window
flutters in my hand

boarded-up cabin
only a shaft of sunshine
can enter

suddenly . .
on the flat Pacific
the sun rolls off

the broom hesitates
almost like grandma's tatting
this spider web

first clap of thunder
our ferocious watchdog
crawls under the bed

Fourth of July storm
the fireworks display canceled
-- thunder and lightning

as the tide rolls in
smoothing every grain of sand
sand castle crumbles

down the mountain road
serpentine of red tail-lights
ending the weekend

osprey penthouse
a tree-top view of the lake
high-rent district

summer breeze moving
graceful limbs of the beech tree
in three-quarter time

over-ripe peach
peeling itself
in my hand

high school reunion
here in the yearbook   the way
I still see him

darting   hovering
your wings never seem to rest
little hummingbird

fly away sparrow
as you search for your breakfast
so does the cat

painting more detail
  on the wisteria bloom
. . . the rising sun

from the canoe
lake mirrors the morning
. . . my head in the clouds

in the rainforest
the sun finds a waterfall
and spins a rainbow

on top of the hill
the lighted cross and full moon
sharing the darkness

five years now
on the answering machine
  still his voice

purple-stained palms
    as she takes her change
        huckleberries ripe

over a hot stove
trying to preserve summer
    in a jar

inchworm crawling
    the length of the snake grass
        measuring the day

the little boy's sox
not long out of the dryer
    lie wet by the door

in dense wilderness
where no man has ever stood
    then   a cola can

that yellow stuff
from the butterfly's wings
   on his hands

                       kindly mending
                 the decaying lattice fence
                           wisteria vine

five o'clock whistle
old man trudging up the road
   dragging his shadow

                 on our boogie boards
             trying to catch a big wave
                 and our youth

artificial blooms
decorating the grave
of this real person

in darkness   rain came
watering the begonias
snuffing out the stars

waiting for the light
traffic sounds racing off with
. . . our conversation

in conversation
all she ever seems to hear
. . . is her own voice

in sacred wetlands
guarding against intruders
mosquito patrol

at the beach cottage
an old cook stove reheating
yesterday's sunburn

porch companions
cricket's chirp   squeaking rocker
the evening star

in a half-dream
 the aroma of coffee
  . . . invading

that's it old frog
what reflects in the water
   is what you are

swimming hole's cool floor
logic says its silty mud
   toes know its velvet

silver shimmerings
flutter under the porch lamp
   ballet of night moth

country road
      smell of peppermint
            and cow dung

sailboat's mast reflects
      in the undulating lake
      . . .   zigzaggedly

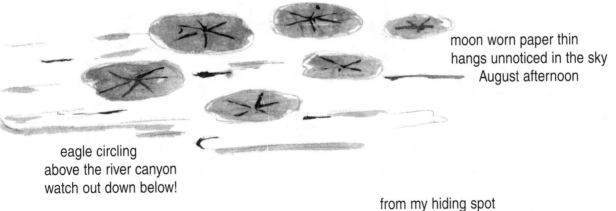

moon worn paper thin
      hangs unnoticed in the sky
            August afternoon

eagle circling
above the river canyon
watch out down below!

from my hiding spot
blue heron clawing a rock
fishing the ripples

sweeping sandy floor
wet hair cooling
sunburned shoulders

shadows lengthening
with sand buckets and sunburns
they desert the beach

the wind whistling
leaves dancing   flowers bowing
a garden party

the teddy bear
just where he dropped it
waits for him   too

the weighty problem
suddenly seems trivial
. . . a white cane groping

uninvited
creeping in the doorway
evening shadows

call of the loon
to which there is no answer
a chilling breeze

blazing sun
resting on the endless sea
extinguished by waves

a splash in the dark
in the lake draped in moon glow
some skinny dippers

an old dog watching
children on their way to school
then closes his eyes

crayon masterpiece
a picture of his mother
. . . with her many arms

in the attic trunk
some seventy-eight records
platform dancing shoes

this familiar place
I find myself holding hands
with old memories

a bristlecone pine
growing out of a rock crag
. . and thriving

some red plum leaves
decorating the pine tree
rushing the season

the first killing frost
too late the white butterfly
visits the garden

an old barn owl
looking like a stuffed toy
then his eyes move

sudden intrusion
neighbor's porch light clicking on
killing the sunrise

air so crispy cold
brings a flush to the oak tree
and little girl's cheeks

in the pine forest
sudden darkness swallowing
the night owl's screech

to understand her
is working the puzzle
without the box top

the lake lies quiet
speedboats gone to storage now
. . . listen to it sigh

Surrounding
Guilin

mountains
I always
thought were

artists'
fantasies

there are no mountains only molehills

at the jazz festival
white-haired man hangs up his cane
to dance with his wife

once we danced
cheek to cheek   now it's
belly to belly

canning apricots
watching the little squirrel
storing some walnuts

echo in the woods
chipping at the silence
a woodcutter's ax

reflections
doubling the aspen
on the far shore

a hard winter freeze --
like magic   blankets appear
at the mission door

while discussing Mom
and her failing memory
we can't find the car

robin on the wire
fluffing up --he tucks his neck
the temperature drops

2 am
exaggerating the cat
its shadow

that magical space
where swarms of sand swallows
don't collide

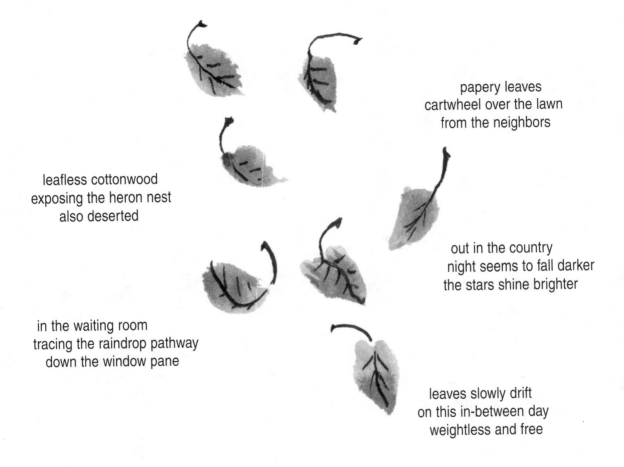

papery leaves
cartwheel over the lawn
from the neighbors

leafless cottonwood
exposing the heron nest
also deserted

out in the country
night seems to fall darker
the stars shine brighter

in the waiting room
tracing the raindrop pathway
down the window pane

leaves slowly drift
on this in-between day
weightless and free

angry clouds
porch floor comes alive
fluttering leaves

pain of surgery
and flowers of condolence
fading together

not quite alone
in this deserted cornfield
a scarecrow

an amber leaf
curling inward to grasp
the last of summer

among gold pieces
a few shiny pennies
mountain aspen

so late coming home
unlocking the front door
releasing darkness

leaves beneath the elm
making a shadow pattern
reflect yesterday

on the barn's roof
owl hangs a jagged wing
across the moon

November second
peeking out of the trash can
a grinning pumpkin

maple tree stands bare --
the scent of deep November
permeates the air

in darkness of night
quiet as a thief it came
the season's first snow

a pewter sky
wedge of geese turning south
white feathers fall

driving blind friend home
wait at the curb for a light
that never turns on

his duties finished
under a blanket of snow
a scarecrow sleeps

as the haze burns off
diamonds sparkle in the snow
   left over star-dust

        by the wood stove
        deep into Michener
        . . . wintering

    planting sack of bulbs
      settling for the fact
        won't remember where

        in throwing bread crumbs
          charity insists sparrow
            hungry as the wren

as the sun goes down
this new-fangled sensor light
   turns on like the moon

       Moriah growls   barks!
        then races to the front door
          to wag her tail

neighbor's curtains drawn
reaching in the mailbox
. . . a rejection slip

a brisk autumn walk
leaves crackle like cornflakes
as hands find pockets

geese honk on the beach
announce the flight going south
like at the airport

it can't be that long
moss shrouding the name   the dates
on the epitaph

an abrupt cold snap
hot dog vender dancing
to keep his feet warm

above the fog
mountain peak collecting light
valley disappears

a warm chinook wind
leaves imprinted on the walk
fossils of summer

last year's calendar
and a clock that isn't wound
on the old man's desk

flat cloud shadows
hover above the foothills
deepening color

raining greyness
dead world   no sign of life
smell the sweet of green

thumbing pages
sensing the antiquity
by the book's odor

from high in the tree
into the bathroom window
a squirrel peeking

buttoning her coat
she picks the last of the mums
in a snow storm

giving relief
to the total white-out
a red barn

at the rummage sale
smile on the old lady's face
when the jacket fits

SCOTLAND -- "HASTE YE BACK"

buried
in ancient castle ruins
spirit of the Scots

at the pubs
welcome as the local folk
sheep dogs

sagging ground
surrounds the village kirk
heavy with tombstones

from gilded frames
outrageous tartan kilts
determined faces

baby carriages
outside the village shops
unattended

August raindrops
spatting gently to the earth
sparkle in the sun

filling the air
flock of mourning doves
the drone of bagpipes

castle turret
disappearing
in the mist

SOUTH AMERICAN TRAVELOG

still blue water
jungle beat of the samba
   in Rio

in the twilight
a stranger stepping into
   my shadow

from the plane
miles of the rainforest
   waterfalls

  Iguacu Falls
where it is ordinary
  to see rainbows

it's always summer
risking water on their wings
   butterflies

beneath our feet
serene lagoon fall
                ing
into another
           fall

a macaw cries
pathway slippery slick
   a mongoose

above the falls
walk the wooden bridge
  nervous laughter

feeling the pulse
of the Argentine
in sexy tango

in the Falklands
what good are umbrellas
blown inside out?

56

rough swells of the sea
monument to lost sailors
around the Horn

Magellan Strait
wind-patterned water
redundant sky

in Chacabuco
choosing handicrafter's ware
her smile

remote Puerta Montt
bright-eyed boys offer
flowers

curious children
come and talk to us
without fear

Valparaiso
bushes of hibiscus
hide the graffiti

language barrier
reaching beyond it
exchanging smiles

landing in Cuzco
moss covering Inca ruins
a Shangri-la

wedged between Andes
Uribamba River
spitting white water

thin mystic air
lost in the ethereal
Machu Picchu

rensaku sequence*

A PILGRIMAGE

Protestants
joining Catholics
a Jewish guide

loving the rhythm
hold hands with strangers
a folk dance

open-air cafe
the flavor of Israel
falafels

shrill Arabic chant
Moslems called to prayer
from distant towers

sea of Galilee
St. Peter's fish stares up
from my dinner plate

between two stones
insert my written prayer
in the Wailing Wall

by the sea
Church of Beatitudes
as is was then

Mount of Olives
shepherds tending sheep
a Christmas card

ancient stone jars
Cana   the first miracle
water to wine

taking turns
carrying the wood cross
climb cobbled streets

ninth station
stopped by machine guns
security tension

windy desert
faces covered, tents, camels
black-eyed bedouins

stained glass windows
the 12 tribes of Israel
rainbows on the pews

mosques   synagogues
churches   testimony to
man's need to believe

Jewish night club
male Barbra Striesand sings
I fall in love

Friday night
guide stops for flowers
tradition

Jewish men
curled side locks
in kapotes

above the dead sea
rises steeply   looms bleakly
Masada

new excavation
layer under layer
exposed to the sun

7th century
mosaic floor reads:
"PEACE UPON ISRAEL"

*Footnote: (rensaku sequence: a group of haiku not intended to stand alone--each contributes to the whole.)